Extemporization for Music Students

by

REGINALD HUNT

Music Department

OXFORD UNIVERSITY PRESS

44 CONDUIT STREET, LONDON, W.1

1968

To my Friend
Dr. W. S. Lloyd Webber
Director of the London College of Music

CONTENTS

Examples are numbered consecutively throughout. *Exercises* are numbered afresh as they appear in each chapter.

INTRODUCTION

Extemporization is a vast subject which formerly played a bigger part in music making than is the case now. Musicians are no longer expected to be able to construct whole movements, including fugues, from the scanty material supplied. However, extemporization still enters into musical activity on a modest, incidental scale, and a player who cannot make a convincing shot at it, when the need arises, is by that token something less than an all-round musician.

Extemporization today may be classified under three main heads:
(1) That involving definite form, modulation, and some development of theme. (2) That conceived almost entirely on a rhythmic basis (e.g. in the Dalcroze Eurhythmic system). (3) That used by jazz performers, consisting mainly of one-dimensional melodic and rhythmic embroidery superimposed by a soloist on a fixed harmonic basis. This course deals with the first type only.

Occasions for Extemporization

Extemporization is particularly important for organists. The organist is often called upon to fill up gaps in the church service and must be able to extemporize if awkward hitches are to be avoided: without this facility the player will tend to 'fill in' with a bit of his favourite 'doodling' —a stock passage nearly always the same and showing no musical connection with what comes before and after. Too often an organist of this type will be insufficiently keen or competent to play a worth-while piece as a concluding voluntary, and will 'improvise' something to see the congregation out of the church—to the exasperation of musical listeners unable to get out quickly enough. Even at its best extemporization should be used only when necessary and appropriate: the considered thoughts of a composer as set forth in a finished work will almost always be on a higher plane than an improvisation, which by its very nature is ephemeral.

It is also one of the essential skills for a teacher of class music—for instance, to provide the prelude to a folk-song when the printed voice part starts straight away in the first bar; to produce music which illustrates a rhythm in a lesson on music and movement; to demonstrate modulation and its possibilities; to explain all sorts of musical points as they occur, without the time-wasting necessity to hunt through books and sheet music for examples.

At examinations in music it is probable that extemporization is feared most of all the practical tests that plague candidates. Sight reading is a matter of reproducing correctly what is before their eyes; score reading calls for the ability to do much the same thing with the parts more spread out, along with some transposition; transposition requires the ability to read printed melody and harmony and convert these into another key. In all these tests there is always something tangible before the candidate. However, in extemporization the candidate sees in front of him a figure, motive, or complete phrase, on which he must construct a piece of his own. He is launched upon an uncharted sea, completely dependent on his musicianship, presence of mind, and the ability to remember what he begins with. He is required to invent harmony, to exploit and develop the given material, to continue in the style indicated, to clothe his thoughts in coherent form, not to meander and lose the thread of his discourse, and above all never to come to a full stop until the music has been brought to a satisfactory conclusion. No wonder that many students never manage to show any facility in this exacting process, much less give a convincing performance. (It should be added that most examiners are indulgent in marking this test, having become resigned to a moderate standard.)

Scope and Purpose of the Course

This course is intended first and foremost to help musicians to pass examination tests in this most difficult art. To have any hope of success it must lay down principles and make recommendations. It is therefore bound to be concerned with a more or less stereotyped and rigid form. Without such rigid support the average student will be lost and his attempt to improvise will founder: in the atmosphere of emotional tension inseparable from examination conditions thoughts do not flow freely, and lacking the practised discipline of a plan the candidate's attempt is likely to result in disaster. Even with this help the tests are difficult enough; without a plan or framework extemporization is all the more daunting.

Specifically, the aim of the course is to help students to pass the extemporization tests which form part of the examinations for the Graduate, School Music, and Organ diplomas of the musical colleges, including the Royal College of Organists. The tests may be put in three groups:

(1) Extemporization in the simplest ternary form, consisting of the addition of a responsive phrase to a given harmonized phrase (making an eight-bar sentence), followed by a middle sentence of the same length in a contrasted key, and concluding with the repetition of the first sentence: twenty-four bars in all with perhaps a short coda.
This type is expected from candidates for some School Music diplomas.

(2) Extemporization following the harmonization at sight of a melody of folk-song or similar nature, the extemporization consisting mainly of the development of material from the melody harmonized. This type is expected from candidates for most Graduate and some Organ diplomas.

(3) Extemporization in a more extended ternary form than in (1) above and based on a given theme rather than a complete phrase, usually melody only.
This type is expected from candidates for the highest Organ diplomas, though the Royal College of Organists does not mention any particular type in its examination regulations.

Details of the various requirements of examining bodies are given in the Appendix.

Other Considerations

For the purposes of this book it is assumed that the music student has followed a course of ear-training and has acquired by training what is generally described as musicianship, and that he has a good knowledge of the piano keyboard. In more specific terms: he should have studied harmony well beyond the dominant seventh, the use of unessential notes, and modulation to related keys; he should understand binary and ternary form and elementary development of a theme; and he should be able to anticipate the probable shape of a melody and remember what has already been played.

In harmonization tests at the keyboard 'vocal' harmony in four parts is expected as a rule. In extemporization, however, instrumental considerations apply, as in pianoforte and organ writing: there will be complete freedom as to the number of parts, which may vary from bar to bar, less than four or more according to the player's fancy. In examinations it is best not to be venturesome—either in the excessive use of discord or in modulation to remote keys. Great originality is not expected. The candidate will be fully extended in managing traditional harmony, even well-worn clichés and modulation to nearly related keys. Examiners mostly look for coherence or shape.

The student who finds great difficulty in achieving fluency in these tests should practise writing down his or her thoughts. There is quite a close analogy between musical improvisation and public speaking. Many fluent speakers—now able to 'think on their feet'—reached this happy state only after a long apprenticeship, during which their thoughts had to be painfully assembled on paper. This preliminary assembling on paper is equally useful when learning to 'think at the keyboard'.

The justification for the inclusion of extemporization tests in examinations is surely that they should help the musician to develop his skill in this exacting and difficult art. It is to be hoped that from the limited beginnings outlined in this book the young musician will be encouraged to experiment and launch out on free and spontaneous extemporization on a wider and more artistic basis.

CHAPTER I

Adding a Four-Bar Non-modulating Responsive
Phrase to a Given Four-Bar Statement Phrase

In this first stage the given (statement) phrases are all in regular four-bar rhythm and finish on a note of the tonic chord. The non-modulating responsive phrases, though differing melodically, are to repeat the rhythm of the statement phrases and finish on the tonic itself.

The length of a phrase is determined by the number of first beats of the bar, ignoring any notes at the beginning or end of the phrase. In this chapter all the first beats of bars are indicated by numbers in brackets.

In this square-cut regular rhythmic style the pattern of the first phrase is reflected in the pattern of the second: thus, if the first phrase begins on the first beat of the bar, the second phrase will do likewise. Similarly a second-beat beginning in the first phrase will be reflected by a second-beat beginning in the second phrase, a third beat by a third beat, and so on.

Consider the following examples:

In Ex. 1 both phrases begin on the first beat of the bar in 4/4 time. In Ex. 2 both phrases begin on the third beat of the bar in 3/4 time. In Ex. 3 both phrases begin on the second beat of the bar in 4/4 time, the first three crotchets belonging rhythmically to the bar which follows.

6

Ex.1

Statement phrase   Response

|1| |2| |3| |4| |1| |2| |3| |4|

Ex. 2

Statement   Response

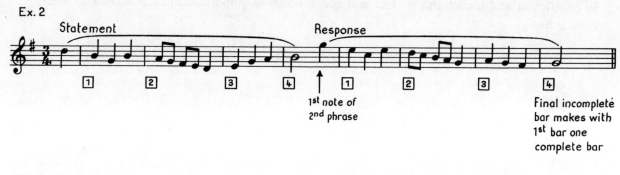

|1| |2| |3| |4| |1| |2| |3| |4|

1st note of   Final incomplete
2nd phrase   bar makes with
                     1st bar one
                     complete bar

Ex. 3

Statement   Response

|1| |2| |3| |4| |1| |2| |3| |4|

                     Making with
                     1st bar one
                     complete bar

Harmonization of Exx. 1-3. Passing notes are used freely to reduce the number of chords.

Ex.1a

|1| |2| |3| |4| |1| |2| |3| |4|

Although four-part harmony is used, the player will often find it convenient to take three notes with the right hand and one with the left, as in Exx. 2 and 3 below.

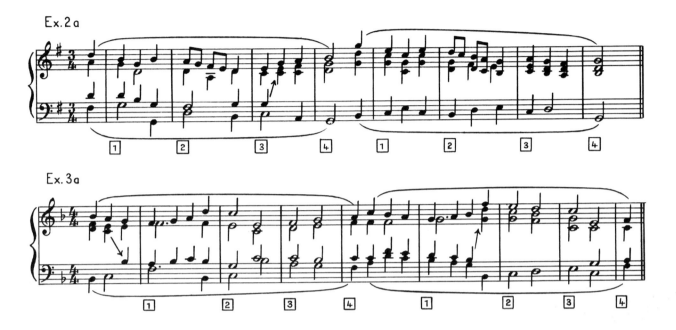

EXERCISES ON CHAPTER I

(*a*) Play the given phrases, melody only, and add responsive phrases in exactly the same rhythm, finishing on the tonic.

(*b*) Repeat, harmonizing the phrases at the keyboard.

(*c*) As soon as facility is obtained, the first stage (melody only) should be omitted.

(*d*) Where a phrase is indicated as a two-bar phrase, the response should be of that length.

(*e*) In each case, phrase the music as if reading from a copy bearing appropriate phrase-marks.

Students finding difficulty in working these exercises at the keyboard should begin by making preliminary sketches on paper, discarding this step as soon as possible.

8

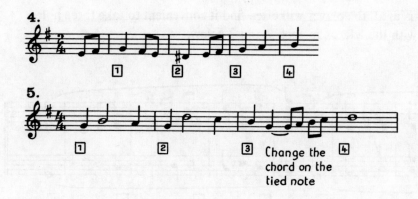

6.

Siciliano

(Harmonized)

CHAPTER II

Adding a Modulating Responsive Phrase to a Given Phrase

To save space the examples are shown as already harmonized, unessential notes being freely employed. The second phrase in each case repeats the rhythmic pattern of the first. While the first phrase in Ex. 4 remains in the tonic key of A minor, the second modulates to C, the relative major. The first phrase in Ex. 5 is in F major and the second ends in the dominant, C major. The first in Ex. 6 is entirely in A, while the second modulates to E, the dominant, Ex. 7 has its first phrase in E flat, the first A natural being an auxiliary note; the second phrase modulates to the dominant, B flat.

Ex. 4 `- - - - - - Given - - - - - -`

Moderato

Note. As the modulation implies a continuation of the melody after the
second phrase, the last bar of the example is left without double bar.

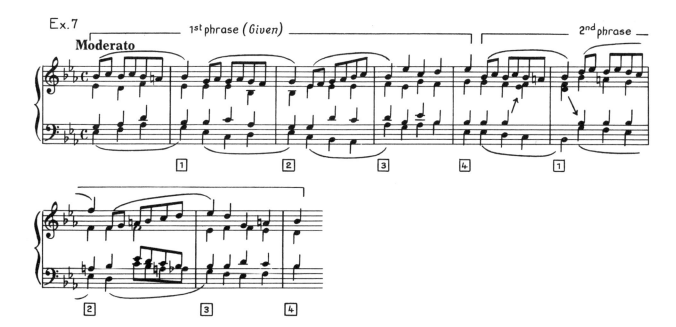

10

EXERCISES ON CHAPTER II

Complete at the keyboard the harmonization of the following phrases. Then add harmonized responsive phrases, modulating to the dominant in the case of major melodies and to the relative major when the first phrase is in a minor key. The main phrase is now indicated by a square bracket; curves and other marks are used for subsidiary phrasing inside the main phrase.

1.

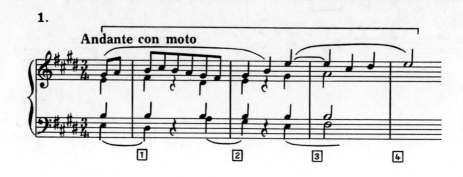

2.

3.

4.

5.

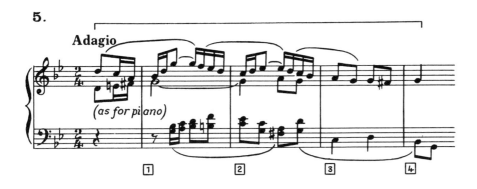

6.

Start of
2nd phrase

7.

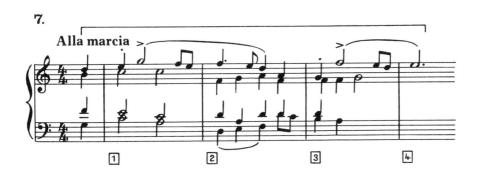

12

CHAPTER III

**Adding a Responsive Phrase (continued)—Opening Phrases which
Modulate—Modifying the Rhythm in the Second Phrase**

The following examples illustrate variations from the modulatory scheme used up to the present.

In Ex. 8 the first phrase modulates to the dominant key, and the second returns to the tonic.

In Ex. 9 the first (minor) phrase modulates to the dominant minor, with Picardy Third, instead of the relative major, while the second phrase passes through the subdominant minor (G minor) before returning to the tonic.

In Ex. 10 the opening major phrase modulates to the dominant, while the second passes through the subdominant major and its relative minor (E flat minor) before returning to the tonic.

These examples continue to use the same rhythmic pattern for both phrases. Ex. 11, however, does not do this exactly, but finishes with a long note on the first beat of the last bar. Its modulatory scheme is: first phrase minor, second phrase relative major.

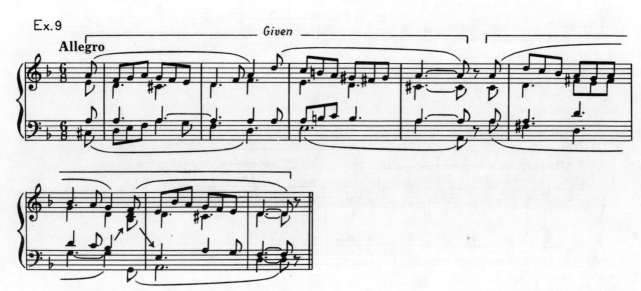

Note on how to determine the Length of Phrases. The student may be puzzled to decide whether a phrase covers two bars or four. Many passages may be interpreted as consisting either of two phrases of four bars each or four phrases of two bars each: there is no hard and fast rule, and the interpretation depends for the most part on the taste and fancy of the person concerned. Exx. 1, 2, 3, 6, 7, 9, and 10 could all have been divided into four phrases of two bars each. However, the *tempo* and the number of *short notes* (quavers and semiquavers) should be the deciding factors. These examples were all taken to be in quick tempo: Exx. 1, 2, 3, and 10 also have few notes shorter than a crotchet. Hence a longish phrase is appropriate for them. Exx. 6 and 9 have plenty of quavers, and if played at a slow tempo would be better with four phrases.

If Exx. 9 and 11 are compared, it will be noticed that the former is marked 'Allegro' and the latter 'Andante'; Ex. 9 has no note shorter than a quaver, but Ex. 11 has many semiquavers. The reason for the different rhythmic analysis will be plain.

Ex. 7 is a border-line case; there is much continuous quaver movement, and the four-bar phrasing might be thought too long. It is a matter of opinion.

Exercise 6 at the end of Chapter I is marked 'Siciliano', a slow tempo, and therefore the given passage makes a two-bar phrase.

EXERCISES ON CHAPTER III

Complete at the keyboard the harmonization of the given phrase, then continue with another harmonized phrase of the same length. In Exercise I the added phrase should return to the tonic. In Exercise 2 the added phrase should also return to the tonic. Exercise 3 should remain in the relative major, D flat, at the end of four bars; so should Exercise 4, also four bars. The second phrase in each of these exercises might show a little rhythmic difference from the first: No. 3 might conclude with a dotted minim occupying the fourth bar, while the last bar of No. 4 might consist of a minim tied to a quaver.

In Exercises 5 and 6 the added phrase should return to the tonic key.

CHAPTER IV

Adding Three Phrases to a Given Phrase

Previous chapters have been concerned with melodies of two phrases, generally making one sentence. Four-phrase melodies are now to be considered: these may be assumed generally to make a sort of musical paragraph of two sentences. The rigidity of rhythm, and to some extent of modulation, will be somewhat relaxed at times, but the form of these four-phrase passages will always be binary—eight (or four) bars in Part I and eight (or four) bars in Part II.

The *modulatory scheme* suggested to begin with is as follows:

MAJOR KEY

Phrase 1 in the tonic key.

Phrase 2 modulating to the dominant.

Phrase 3 beginning in the subdominant.

Phrase 4 in the tonic.

MINOR KEY

Phrase 1 in the tonic.

Phrase 2 in the relative major (alternatively in the dominant minor).

Phrase 3 beginning in the relative major (or dominant minor) and working back to the tonic.

Phrase 4 in the tonic.

The rhythmic scheme suggested to begin with is as follows:

Phrase 2 in the same rhythm as phrase 1, except for a possible modification in the last bar.

Phrase 3 to consist of a rudimentary development of the more active part of phrase 1, perhaps with sequential repetition.

Phrase 4 in the same rhythm as phrase 1, except for a possible modification of the ending.

This stereotyped plan can of course be dispensed with as soon as facility and confidence have been attained. But one of the main difficulties in extemporization is to remember what has gone before. The adoption of a formal plan will train the memory and lay the foundation for spontaneous and artistic extemporization later on.

To consider the examples which follow; Ex. 12 consists of four phrases of two bars each. Phrase 2 copies the rhythm of phrase 1 in the first bar, but substitutes a long note for the four crotchets in the second bar of phrase 1. Phrase 3 consists of a 'development' of phrase 1, repeating the rhythm of the more active bar 1 (crotchet—triplet quavers—crotchet—crotchet) along with an ascending sequence. Phrase 4 modifies the pattern of phrase 1 like phrase 2.

The modulatory scheme of Ex. 13 is: phrase 1 in the tonic minor; phrase 2 moving to the dominant minor; phrase 3 in the relative major; phrase 4 back in the tonic. Phrases 2 and 4 are rhythmically identical with phrase 1. Phrase 3 develops the rhythm of the second (full) bar of phrase 1, making special use of the group consisting of a quaver and two semiquavers.

Ex. 14 passes from the tonic minor to the relative major in phrase 2; its third phrase moves by means of a sequence through the relative major back to the tonic, making use of the dotted quaver-and-semiquaver figure from phrase 1.

In all the other examples the third phrase develops a figure from the first phrase, the music beginning in each case in the major and working through the dominant and subdominant majors before returning to the original key.

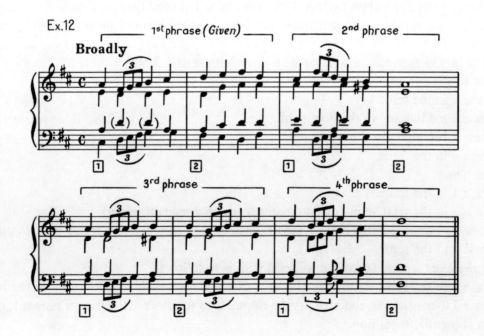

18

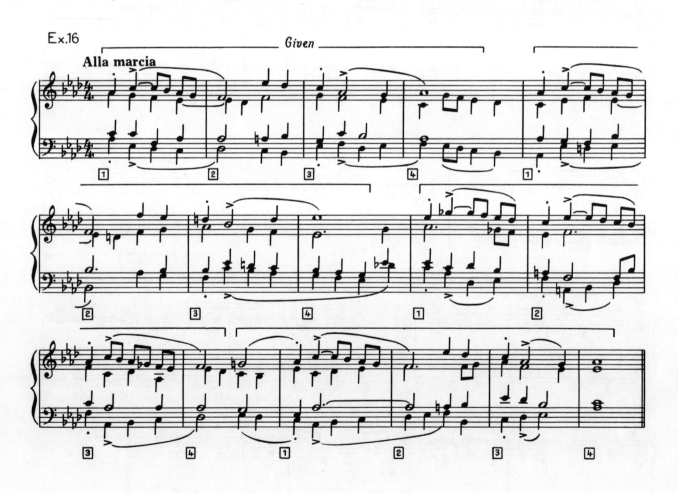

Ex.17

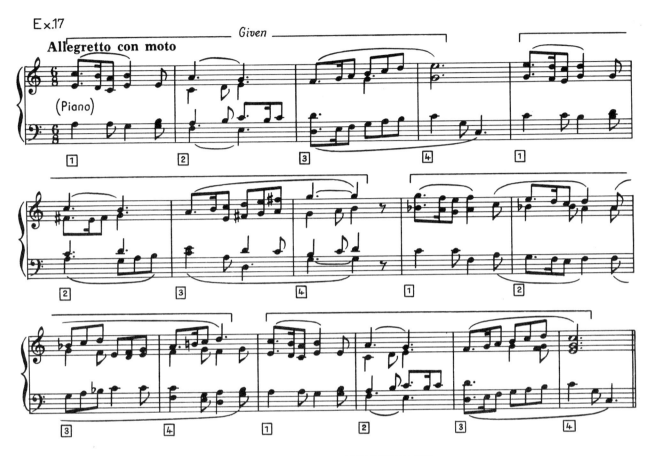

EXERCISES ON CHAPTER IV

(1) *Two-bar phrases.* Starting in each case with the given two-bar phrase, improvise at the keyboard three more phrases, making eight bars in all. Apply the modulatory schemes and rhythmic plans outlined in the chapter. Exercises 1 and 4 should be in piano idiom, i.e., the number of parts should be varied, according to taste: Nos. 2 and 3 should be in four-part harmony throughout.

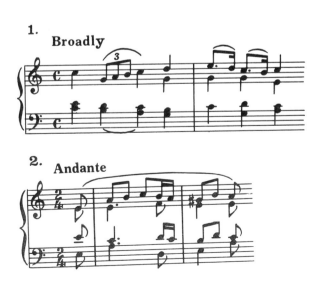

3. Minuet

4. Siciliano

(2) *Four-Bar Phrases*. Starting in each case with a given four-bar phrase, improvise at the keyboard three more phrases, making sixteen bars in all. As in the first four exercises in this chapter, apply the modulatory schemes and rhythmic plans previously outlined, taking Exx. 13, 14, 16, and 17 as models.

Nos. 5, 6, and 10 should be harmonized in pianistic fashion, Nos. 7, 8, and 9 in four-part harmony throughout.

5. Alla marcia

6. Con moto

7. Moderato con brio

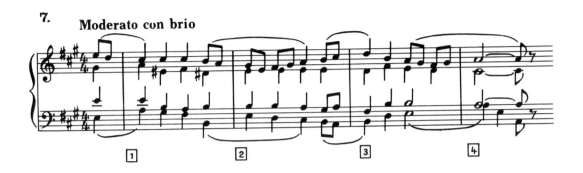

8. Andante con moto

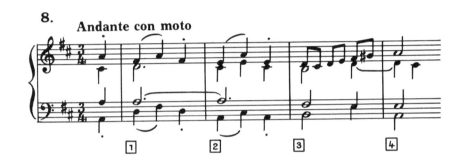

9. Allegretto

10. Risoluto

(3) *More difficult Exercises.* Exercise 11 is based on a four-bar phrase, and the suggested rhythmic plan is as given below:

Exercises 12 and 13 are based on two-bar phrases, and the suggested rhythmic plans are supplied.

13. Moderato

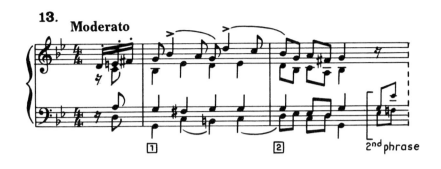

Phrases 1 & 2

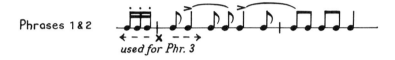

used for Phr. 3

Phrase 3

Phrase 4 ~ *like 1 (or slightly modified)*

(4) *Phrases of which only the Melody is Given.* Exercises 14-19 each consist of a given phrase of two-bar length, which is to be harmonized and followed by three more two-bar phrases, making a harmonized passage of eight bars in all.

Exercises 20-25 each consist of a given phrase of four-bar length, which is to be harmonized and followed by three more four-bar phrases, making a harmonized passage of sixteen bars in all.

CHAPTER V

**Extemporization on a Less Rigid Pattern of Four Phrases—
Imitative Openings—Varying the Number of Harmonic Parts**

The plan recommended in Chapter IV involved in almost every case repeating the rhythm and melody of the first or second phrase, with very little alteration, to form the fourth phrase. As explained in the Introduction, a stereotyped plan supplies the candidate with a sort of sheet-anchor to steady him in examination conditions. However, students interested in the subject from the artistic as well as from the examination point of view would do well to experiment occasionally, taking folk-songs as models.

It is for the individual student to decide whether a rigid plan or a freer one is to be relied upon in examination work. But it is advisable to be adventurous in modulation rather than in rhythm —that is, the sixteen-bar framework and the admittedly square rhythm should be retained. Once the rhythmic character of the given phrase or theme has been lost, incoherence sets in and the player simply flounders.

In Ex. 18 the regular four-bar pattern is maintained, but the second phrase modulates to the mediant minor, not the dominant major or relative minor. The first, second, and fourth phrases all differ in some respect, both melodically and rhythmically. The unifying characteristic is the syncopated figure, marked 'x', which appears in all three of those phrases. The sequence in the third phrase would aid memorization, but on the whole the player would find it very hard to recall what he had played in the first sixteen bars, if they formed the first part of an improvisation in ternary form. Ternary form is dealt with in a later chapter, where it will be seen how important a part memorization plays in the final section of A B A form.

Ex. 19 is unified rhythmically by the opening figure of four semiquavers followed by two quavers and a crotchet: in the last phrase the semiquavers are run together in a final flourish. The melody has a descending seventh as a prominent feature. The modulatory scheme includes a progression to the relative minor in phrase 1, to the dominant major and mediant minor in phrase 2, and to the subdominant major in phrase 4, which is largely based on a descending sequence.

As exercises in this freer form the student should experiment with the given phrases in exercises 1-25 in Chapter IV, modifying the rhythmic plans formerly used and passing through different keys.

As stated in the Introduction, there should be complete freedom in the number of harmonic parts. If the player is sufficiently bold and confident to begin with the melody alone and then bring in a second part in free imitation, this will introduce an element of variety and enterprise into the extemporization. But such treatment calls for considerable presence of mind, as the player has to decide on the spur of the moment whether the theme or melody is of the type to lend itself to imitation. It will be quite enough just to hint at imitation in the opening bars: to attempt anything more in an extemporization examination would be injudicious.

Six examples which have already appeared in different guise in previous chapters are treated below in this fashion. It should be noticed that the treatment is applied only to the opening phrase, after which the harmony is as before. The indication '(a)' has been added to the original number of the example: thus, '5(a)' is Ex. 5 with a new beginning, and so on.

Ex. 20 shows a simple imitative opening to a phrase which seems to call for such treatment.

Ex. 21 shows an extemporization on the following phrase:-

28

The passage is mainly in two-part harmony.

Ex. 21

Ex. 22 is based on the following phrase:-

Ex. 23 shows the great variation in the number of parts possible in an organ extemporization.
The given phrase is:

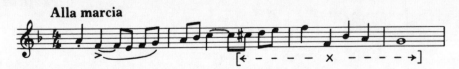

The figure 'x' is developed in the third phrase of the extemporization.

Ex. 23

EXERCISES ON CHAPTER V

On page 25 the student is recommended to experiment with the phrases given in exercises 1-25 in Chapter IV, using a freer rhythmic plan than that given in that chapter.

Of exercises from previous chapters the following may be used for imitative openings:

      Chapter I: Nos. 2 and 5

      Chapter II: No. 1

      Chapter III: No. 6

      Chapter IV: Nos. 4, 24, 25.

Of exercises belonging specifically to this Chapter, Nos. 1-6 are suitable for imitative openings; No. 7 for piano largely in two parts; No. 8 for organ with much variation in the number of parts; and Nos. 9 and 10 for either organ or piano. In each case the figure (--x--) is suitable for exploitation in the third phrase of the extemporization, which, unless otherwise stated, is to be of sixteen-bar length.

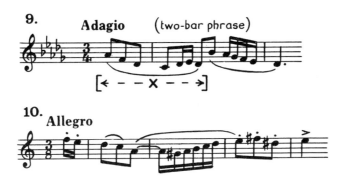

CHAPTER VI

Extemporizing a Short Coda to a Hymn Tune

An organist is often called upon to go on playing when a hymn has finished before the minister or priest is ready to continue and a short 'filling in' is needed. Such codas should generally end softly in order to lead unobtrusively into what follows. There is very seldom any need for an improvisation *before* a hymn, the almost universal custom being to play the first line of the tune at the speed the hymn is to be sung.

Such an extemporization following a hymn tune is one of the requirements of the examinations for organ diplomas granted by two of the London musical colleges.*

Extemporization of this sort should avoid giving the impression that a fresh piece of music is beginning: tune and improvisation should sound continuous. A very useful plan is to begin the original contribution with a tonic pedal and subdominant harmony. Subdominant harmony, however, should not continue beyond a few bars; it exercises such a strong pull that, if persisted in, it will usurp the position of the legitimate tonic, and make the ultimate return of the latter sound like a modulation to the dominant. One should move away from the subdominant as soon as possible.

The material of the continuation should consist of a little development or exploitation of what has gone before. The player must have an eye to the more rhythmically alive sections of the hymn or the more striking features of the melody. Hymn tunes tend to be lacking in characteristic rhythm, one of the exceptions being 'Monkland', which has a mixture of minims and crotchets (or crotchets and quavers, according to whether the hymnal gives the time signature as 4/2 or 4/4) and the contrast of alternating common chord arpeggios and scale passages.

---

* L.L.C.M. (Organ) (transposition of the given tune precedes the extemporization), and L.T.C.L. and F.T.C.L. (Organ).

'Monkland' is in the key of C, which requires the congregation to attempt the top E in the last line. One of the organ tests referred to in the footnote includes the transposition of the given tune before the start of the extemporization. In Ex. 24 therefore the tune is first written in C major, the section for development in the coda being marked. Then, to save space, the last line is written in B flat major, as if the whole tune had been transposed a tone down. After a short pause to mark the ending of the hymn, the organ proceeds to subdominant harmony on a tonic pedal.

In this freer type of extemporization there is much less need to remember what has gone before, while in developing a figure or melodic shape, square four-bar rhythm no longer applies.

Ex. 25 is a coda to the hymn tune 'Winchester Old', the most active feature of which is the dotted minim in the first and third phrases, while the most prominent melodic feature is the descending scale in the third phrase. Both these characteristics have been used in the extemporization, together with the first three notes of the fourth phrase. The tonic pedal link has been interpreted not as the bass of a 6/4 chord on the subdominant but as the third in the chord of the flattened submediant (first inversion of the triad on D flat).

Ex. 25 'Winchester Old'

With a smooth, even tune such as 'Rockingham', which has no active rhythmic pattern, a sequential treatment of some part of the melody will probably take the place of any figure development. In Ex. 26 the coda to the hymn tune begins with the original first phrase put into the subdominant, and this is followed by a sequence built on the second phrase. The repeated notes in the original second phrase are tied in the extemporization and treated as real suspensions. After this use of the second phrase, the coda is brought to an end by two appearances of the fourth phrase.

34

Ex. 26   'Rockingham'

In Ex. 27—a coda to the hymn tune 'Aus der Tiefe' ('Forty days and forty nights')—it should be observed that a convenient way of introducing the subdominant continuation in a minor key is to sharpen the third of the tonic chord, giving a Picardy Third effect: but more than one note (F sharp for F natural) should be changed. The tonic chord of D minor therefore changes to the tonic seventh, which, besides requiring F sharp, brings in C natural for C sharp (the leading note of D minor).

This extemporization leads off with phrase 1 in the subdominant, followed by phrase 2 in the tonic. Phrase 3 follows, modulating to the submediant major (B flat), then appearing again in sequence in the tonic key. To finish, phrase 4 is used twice with varied harmony.

EXERCISES ON CHAPTER VI

As already mentioned, hymn tunes as a general rule are not remarkable for distinctive rhythm, many of them being successions of whole-beat notes, usually minims or crotchets, with occasional half-beat notes, crotchets or quavers respectively. Some tunes, however, are freer in style, with numbers of unessential half-beat notes. These present more material for development, but are more difficult to harmonize satisfactorily than the more sedate tunes. Nevertheless, the student should persevere with them because of the opportunities they give.

The following tunes fall into this category: 'Carlisle', 'Morning Hymn' (Barthélémon), 'Shipston', 'St. Stephen', 'Sussex', 'Bishopthorpe', 'Truro', 'Irish', 'Duke Street'.

Flowing tunes like 'Wareham', 'Wiltshire', 'Richmond' and 'Abridge'—all in triple time— give plenty of scope for extemporization.

Some six-line tunes—for example, 'Dix', 'St. Denio', 'Neander'— are really four-phrase tunes, as the first two phrases are repeated.

Organists should attempt other good tunes lacking movement, such as 'Bristol', 'Merton' 'Innocents', 'Stuttgart', 'Dundee', 'Culbach', 'Albano', 'Old Hundredth', 'Cape Town', 'St. Peter', 'Tallis's Ordinal', 'St. Bernard', 'Hursley', 'St. Fulbert', 'Lincoln', 'Metzler's Redhead' (No. 66), 'St. Magnus' (Nottingham), 'University College', 'Palms of Glory', 'St. Anne', 'Franconia', 'St. Alphege', 'Nativity' (Lahee).

The player should of course not limit himself to four-line tunes.

CHAPTER VII

Extemporizing a Prelude and Coda to a Melody in Folk-Song Idiom

As most folk-songs begin immediately with the voice part, the function of a prelude is to set the tempo and to bring in the voice conveniently; the prelude must therefore be in strict time throughout. It may consist of one of the phrases of the song, generally the first or last four bars—modifying the ending of the phrase to finish on the dominant chord or a chord convenient to the entry of the voice. Alternatively the prelude may be constructed on some striking figure from the tune, so arranged as to lead naturally to the entry of the voice. This kind of prelude may be described in the examination requirements for one diploma as a simple lead-in to a folk-song type of melody.*

The coda, however, will be longer (about sixteen bars) and, as with the hymn in Chapter VI, should introduce some degree of development of the tune. In Ex. 28, 'Jock o' Hazeldean', the four-bar prelude consists of the first phrase of the tune with a modified ending. The coda leads off with a tonic pedal, above which appears the first phrase of the tune in the subdominant key. Phrase 3 follows in the tonic, its most active bar (marked '--x--', with the triplet quaver figure) being used for development. Phrase 4, with its penultimate bar drawn out in length, concludes the extemporization. In simple improvisation it is common practice to conclude with a restatement of the final phrase of the original.

* A.R.C.M. (School Music)

Ex. 28

In Ex. 29, 'Begone, dull care', the prelude again uses phrase 1 of the tune. The coda has no tonic pedal, but phrase 1 still appears in the subdominant. This is followed by a sequence built on the rhythm of the two bars at the end of the first phrase, passing through A minor (supertonic minor) back to the tonic. A development of the first two bars of phrase 4 (rhythm of the words of the second verse) begins on the tonic seventh and works back to the dominant seventh; the triplet quavers are then allowed to run on to a free ending.

Ex. 29

'Begone, dull care'

Ex. 30 shows a prelude and coda to 'The Bailiff's Daughter of Islington'. The prelude of four bars is based on the jaunty dotted quaver and semiquaver figure from the first phrase, followed by the short second phrase ending on the dominant. The coda at first exploits the same figure on a tonic pedal, then modulates to C major. As this jerky figure becomes monotonous after a few repetitions, the extemporization then introduces the third phrase of the tune in C major, then in C minor, working back to the tonic, E flat, when phrase 4—repeated—takes over to finish.

Ex. 31 treats Ex. 13 from Chapter IV in the same style as the three folk-songs mentioned above, a four-bar prelude and a coda being added. The Picardy Third is utilized as the link between tune and improvised coda in order to facilitate the transition to subdominant harmony.

The little figure from the third phrase of the original example (13)—consisting of a quaver and two semiquavers—is given prominence in the coda and changes naturally into running semi-quavers.

EXERCISES ON CHAPTER VII

The exercises are divided into the following groups:

(1) Improvising preludes and codas to specified folk-songs and national songs to be found in standard collections. For these exercises 'melody' editions should be used.

(2) Improvising codas to examples from previous chapters of this book.

(3) Transposing a hymn tune in four parts and continuing with an extemporization on material from the tune.

(4) Harmonizing melodies at the keyboard and continuing with an extemporization as in (3).

(1) The following melodies are suggested for treatment:

'Barbara Allen', 'The British Grenadiers', 'Early one morning', 'The Vicar of Bray', 'Farewell, Manchester', 'Polly Oliver', 'Afton Water', 'Kelvin Grove', 'Robin Adair', 'Ye Banks and Braes', 'The Girl I left behind Me', 'All through the Night'; and these as found in the *Oxford Song Book I*: 'The Ash Grove', 'The Banks of Allan Water', 'Bonnie Charlie's now awa' ', 'Comin' through the Rye', 'Flowers in the Valley', 'The Lincolnshire Poacher', 'Marching through Georgia', 'The Snowy-breasted Pearl'.

Other suitable tunes include: 'The Wraggle Taggle Gipsies, O', 'The Lark in the Morn', 'Blow Away the Morning Dew', 'The Crystal Spring', 'Dashing Away with a Smoothing Iron', 'Spanish Ladies', and 'Greensleeves'.

(2) Play Ex. 12 and 14-17 in Chapter IV and conclude with a short extemporization in each case.

(3) Exercises 1 and 2, in the form of hymn tunes for organ, are to be transposed down a semitone and linked to a suitable coda.*

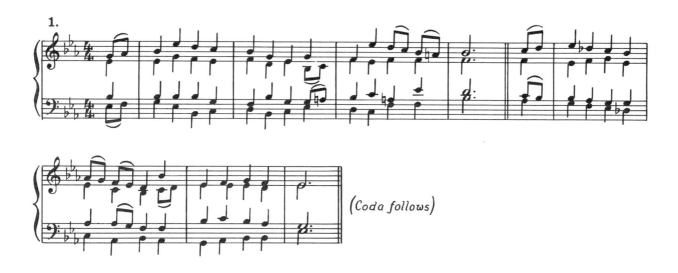

(*Coda follows*)

---

* As for L.L.C.M. (Organ)

42

2.

(Coda follows)

Exercises 3 and 4, passages for piano, are to be transposed down a tone and linked to a suitable coda.

3. **Tempo di minuetto**

(Coda follows)

4. **Andante con moto**

(Coda follows)

(4) In Exercises 5-15 (hymn-like melodies) each passage is to be harmonized at the keyboard and followed by an extemporization based on material from the melody.*

44

Exercises 16-25 are similar to Nos. 5-15, with the difference that the melodies are freer in character and in folk-tune style.*

* G.L.C.M.

46

CHAPTER VIII

Extemporizing on a Theme of less than Phrase Length

Up to this point all the examples and exercises have been in the nature of regular melodies, the given material for improvisation consisting of a complete phrase. This next stage concerns extemporization on a theme which may not be a complete phrase. In such a case it is usual to add to the given theme—to make a complete phrase designed to be the basis of an improvisation.

For instance, an attempt to extemporize on a fragment such as Ex. 32 would result in extreme monotony because of the lack of any rhythmic interest. As the indication 'Allegretto' presupposes a fairly brisk tempo, the extemporization would also be very brief.

This two-bar figure should be extended to four bars, and the added two bars must afford some contrast to the given fragment, thus:

We have now a four-bar phrase on which to build a sixteen-bar passage, as in Ex. 34. From this it will be seen what rhythmic use has been made of the more active (additional) two bars.

The following is a harmonization of Ex. 34. The tied E flat and the corresponding B flat in the second phrase obviously need to be treated as real suspensions.

Ex.35

Ex. 32 called for expansion into a four-bar phrase because it was marked 'Allegretto' and possessed little rhythmic interest. (See Note at the end of Chapter III, dealing with the length of phrases) However, in the case of an 'Adagio' theme in 4/4 time such as Ex. 36, the material for extemporization should be a two-bar phrase (see Ex. 37). A four-bar phrase at that tempo, containing so many quavers and semiquavers, would be difficult to memorize and would produce an inordinately long passage.

Ex. 36

Ex. 37

(*Ex. 36 expanded into a two-bar phrase, the added bar having a different rhythm*)

Ex.38
(Extemporization on the above)
Adagio

EXERCISES ON CHAPTER VIII

Expand the following into two-bar phrases, and harmonize at the keyboard;

1. **Andante pastorale**

2. **Adagio espressivo**

Expand the following into four-bar phrases, and harmonize at the keyboard;

3. **Allegretto scherzando**   (Piano)

4. **Alla marcia**   (Piano)

5. **Sarabande**   (G minor)

6. **Allegro**

7. **Moderato**

8. Alla Siciliana

9. Tempo di Menuetto

10. Gavotte

Each of the above, after expansion, should be used as material for an extemporization of eight or sixteen bars according to the length of phrase indicated.

CHAPTER IX

Extemporizing in Ternary Form

The examples in previous chapters have been either in binary form or in the form of a coda to a melody. Longer extemporizations in the elementary style to which this book is confined will generally be in *ternary* form.

The regulations for one diploma in School Music[1] include an extemporization in very simple style 'of about 24-32 bars in ternary form.' A harmonized phrase of four bars in simple time is put before the candidate, who is asked (a) to add a responsive phrase to the one given (making eight bars for the first section or sentence); (b) to extemporize a middle sentence of eight bars in a contrasted key; to repeat the first eight bars, thus making twenty-four bars in all in A B A form. As a rule a coda is not asked for, though the mention of thirty-two bars does give the candidate scope for this if he wishes to launch out. The middle section, B, need not be remembered.

The above requirement would cover an extemporization on a two-bar phrase and the addition of three more such phrases to make up the A section. However, the custom is to set a four-bar phrase and make the test a very simple affair, as shown in Ex. 39.

Ex. 39 is from the L.L.C.M. School Music Practical Paper, 1966.

(a) Add a responsive phrase to the given phrase making 8 bars.
(b) Extemporize a middle sentence of 8 bars in a contrasted key.
(c) Repeat the first 8 bars—24 bars in all.

1. L.L.C.M. in School Music

Ex. 39

Andante

Alternative ending of (A) (second time) if coda is added:

N.B. Apart from the contrast of key, the crotchet movement in the first phrase of (B) is in its first and third bars, instead of in its second bar as in (A): the contrasted sentence is also a little more active than the first sentence. The given harmony of the opening (variation in the number of parts and single notes in the bass) is a clear indication of piano style.

The extemporization requirements in examinations for standard organ diplomas vary in terminology. One mentions 'an extemporization in ternary form, with coda, on a theme provided'[2]; another stipulates that the attempt should be rhythmical and flowing, 'with some regard for form'[3]; while another calls on the candidate 'to extemporize on one of three themes indicated by the examiners'[4]. The given theme is almost always unharmonized; only very occasionally is a harmonized beginning provided. Whatever the wording of the examination requirement, candidates generally offer an improvisation in ternary form. A complete phrase is hardly ever given, and the theme will require expansion in the manner explained in Chapter VIII. Unless the tempo is very slow, with numerous notes to the bar, Section A will be sixteen bars long.

. 2. F.L.C.M. . 3. L.G.S.M. . 4. F.R.C.O.

52

The major preoccupation in a longer improvisation is the memorization of the A section; hence once again the need for a definite plan. For reasons already gone into, rigidity of plan seems unavoidable if aimless meandering and even complete breakdown are to be ruled out. Examiners look for shape and coherence before everything. Square-cut rhythm and obvious modulations give the candidate confidence and help him through the ordeal. Irksome as so much regimentation must be to the real musician, he or she is recommended to play for safety in examination conditions.

Exx. 40-42 are extemporizations on actual themes set at F.R.C.O. examinations during recent years. The themes are used by kind permission of the Executive Council of the Royal College of Organists. The phrase used in Ex. 39 is quoted by permission of the London College of Music.

For Ex. 40 a two-bar theme, melody only, was given; this, being in 3/4 time and marked 'Allegretto', called for expansion to four-bar length.

In Ex. 40 the theme comes from the F.R.C.O. Practical Paper for July 1965.

The given theme:

The theme extended to 4 bars:

The extemporization for organ:

N.B. Section B is founded on the figure (--x--) which forms the third
bar of Section A.

The material supplied for Ex. 41 consisted of three bars, melody only, in 4/4 time marked
'Andante con moto'; the phrase mark prolonged across the last bar-line of the theme was
interpreted as an invitation to complete the phrase in the added fourth bar. The given key was
B flat, the same as in Ex. 40; this was changed to A for the sake of variety.

54

The theme of Ex. 41 is from the F.R.C.O. Practical Paper for January 1963.

The given theme (original Key B flat):

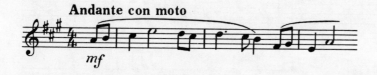

The theme extended to 4 bars:

The extemporization for organ:

Ex.41

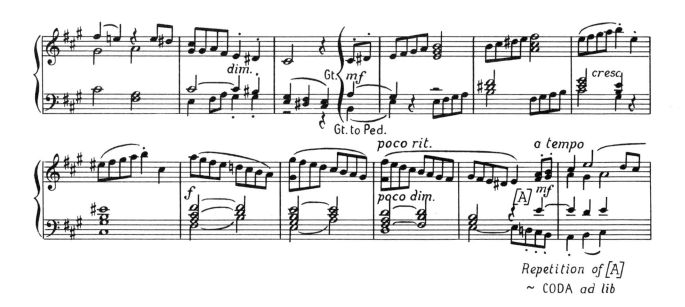

N.B. Section B (in the relative minor of the tonic, A major) is based on the first two quavers of the first bar (incomplete) and the four-quaver figure of the fourth full bar of the opening phrase (--x--). From the relative minor (F sharp) it modulates to the mediant minor (C sharp) before working back to the tonic, A major. It is therefore contrasted in key and in having staccato notes, Section A being legato throughout.

Ex. 42 was to be constructed on two bars marked 'Alla Siciliana', tenor and bass being supplied. The doubling of the treble tied D by the bass D did not lend itself to harmony of any great interest. It seemed legitimate to add another part in the second bar.

The theme of Ex. 42 is from the F.R.C.O. Practical Paper for July 1964.
The given theme:

Alla siciliana

The extemporization for organ (with the theme extended to make a four-bar phrase):

Ex. 42

Alla siciliana

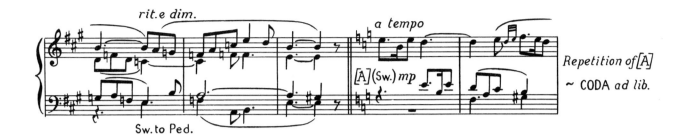

N.B. Section B (in the tonic major, A major) uses the opening figure of Section A (dotted quaver—semiquaver—quaver) followed by a new figure consisting of two detached quavers. The latter is afterwards merged in a legato syncopated figure.

In the above examples (40-42) each middle section, B, though contrasted with A, has some little rhythmic connection with A, this being indicated in the working.

With these examples in ternary form we reach the limits of what is usually expected in examination work. Although in fact we have not even begun to grapple with the many extended shapes and forms that improvisation may cover, this is about as far as one can go on paper. An 'extemporization on paper' represents a contradiction in terms, but there is no other effective way of showing a little of what is possible in this elusive and evanescent art.

EXERCISES ON CHAPTER IX

(1) Extemporizations in the simple style required in certain examinations for diplomas, in which a complete phrase, as distinct from a theme, is supplied.

In addition to the exercises which follow, the student should use material from previous chapters of this course.

From Chapter I

(1) Add responsive phrases to Exercises 1-5, making in each case an eight-bar sentence finishing on the tonic chord.

(2) Extemporize a middle sentence of eight bars in a contrasted key.

(3) Repeat the first eight bars—twenty-four bars in all.

Treat Exercise 6 similarly, sections A and B each consisting of four bars, and the whole occupying twelve bars instead of twenty-four.

From Chapter III

Treat Exx. 8-10 as A sections of ternary extemporizations, and in each case add a contrasted B section.

Treat Exercises 1, 2 and 6 each as opening phrases, add responsive phrases, thus completing eight-bar sentences as section A.

In each case extemporize middle sentences of eight bars in contrasted keys, then repeat A to complete twenty-four bars.

From Chapter IV

Add responsive phrases each of two-bar length to Exercises 1-4, completing sentence A.

Extemporize contrasted sentences (B) each of four-bar length, then repeat A, completing twelve bars in ternary form.

Treat Exercises 6 and 8 as A sentences in ternary form extemporizations each of twenty-four bars.

Treat Exercises 24 and 25 similarly.

Exercises proper to this chapter—Nos. 1-12—should now be worked.

In the form shown in Ex. 39, based on a given phrase of 4 bars, in each case:

(i) Add a responsive phrase to the given phrase making an eight-bar sentence (A):

(ii) Extemporize a middle sentence of eight bars in a contrasted key (B):

(iii) Repeat the first eight bars (A). 24 bars in all. A few bars of coda ad lib.

N.B. In all the above the responsive phrase in Section A must end on the tonic chord, that is (A) must conclude with a perfect cadence in the tonic key. In this shortened form of extemporization there is no scope for a modulation to the dominant in the responsive phrase (Nos. 1, 3 and 5); while in No. 6 the modulation in the given phrase will require the responsive phrase to return to the tonic.

In Nos. 2 and 4 the responsive phrase must not conclude with a modulation to the relative major; though this could be the key of the middle sentence (B).

In the form shown in Ex. 39, based on a given phrase of 2 bars, in each case:

   (i) Add *three* phrases to the given phrase, making 8 bars in all (A):

   (ii) Extemporize a middle section of 8 bars in a contrasted key (B):

   (iii) Repeat the first 8 bars (A). A *few* bars coda ad lib.

(In this connection re-read Chapter IV and refer to Exercises 1-4 in that chapter, which gave practice in adding three 2-bar phrases to a given one of that length).

(2) Extemporizations in the style suitable in examinations for organ diplomas, in which a theme, as distinct from a phrase, is supplied.

Exercises 1-10 at the end of Chapter VIII should be used as bases for extemporizations in ternary form.

   Exercises proper to this chapter—Nos. 13-24—should then be worked.

In the form for Organ shown in Exx. 40-42, extemporize on the following themes, in one or two cases adding a short coda after the repetition of the A section.

60

(a) On the rhythmic basis of a two-bar phrase.

(b) On the rhythmic basis of a four-bar phrase.

APPENDIX

Diploma Examination Requirements

The following English diploma examinations include extemporization as one of their practical tests:-

Royal College of Organists
>   F.R.C.O.

Royal Academy of Music
>   L.R.A.M. (Organ)
>   L.R.A.M. (Aural Training)

Royal College of Music
>   A.R.C.M. (School Music)

Guildhall School of Music
>   G.G.S.M. (Graduate Teacher Diploma)
>   L.G.S.M. (Organ)
>   A.G.S.M. (for Full-Time Students only)

London College of Music
>   G.L.C.M. (Graduate Teacher Diploma)
>   L.L.C.M. (School Music)
>   F.L.C.M. (Organ)
>   L.L.C.M. (Organ)

Trinity College of Music
>   The G.T.C.L. Course includes Extemporization in its 1st and 2nd year, but the subject forms no part of the Final Examination (3rd year).
>   F.T.C.L. (Organ)
>   L.T.C.L. (Organ)
>   L.T.C.L. (Musicianship)

The various requirements are as follows:-

F.R.C.O.: to extemporize on one of three themes indicated by the Examiners.

L.R.A.M. (*Organ*): to extemporize not less than 16 bars on a given theme.

L.R.A.M. (*Aural Training*): to extemporize (in any key) phrases leading up to any required cadence.

A.R.C.M. (*School Music*): to improvise an introduction and harmonize a given melody.

G.G.S.M.: to extemporize on a given theme, in simple style, a short movement such as a Minuet, Gavotte or March, including modulation.

L.G.S.M. (*Organ*): to show a fair facility for simple extemporization of a rhythmical and flowing nature, and with some regard for form.

A.G.S.M.: to improvise a short piece from a given opening, *or* (for singers) to sing an improvised setting of given words.

G.L.C.M.: to harmonize at sight a melody of folk-song or similar nature, and afterwards add a short extemporization on the given tune.

L.L.C.M. (*School Music*): to extemporize about 24-32 bars in ternary form.

F.L.C.M. (*Organ*): to extemporize in ternary form, with coda, on a theme provided by the examiners.

62

L.L.C.M. (*Organ*): to transpose a hymn tune and then to add a coda of about 12 to 16 bars in the style of the hymn tune.

L.T.C.L. (*Organ*): to harmonize a hymn-like melody of eight bars and continue extemporizing for approximately thirty bars, using as material for development a short fragment of the melody indicated by the examiner.

F.T.C.L. (*Organ*): as for L.T.C.L., but the candidate will continue extemporizing on any material derived from the melody.

L.T.C.L. (*Musicianship*): to continue a given harmonic theme in any style or form which the candidate thinks suitable.

:to continue a contrapuntal theme in not more than three parts so as to make a complete piece.